BTEC
BUSINESS
ASSE

Uni

CAROLE TROTTER

HODDER
EDUCATION

AN HACHETTE UK COMPANY

The sample learner answers provided in this assessment guide are intended to give guidance on how a learner might approach generating evidence for each assessment criterion. Answers do not necessarily include all of the evidence required to meet each assessment criterion. Assessor comments intend to highlight how sample answers might be improved to help learners meet the requirements of the grading criterion but are provided as a guide only. Sample answers and assessor guidance have not been verified by Edexcel and any information provided in this guide should not replace your own internal verification process.

Any work submitted as evidence for assessment for this unit must be the learner's own. Submitting as evidence, in whole or in part, any material taken from this guide will be regarded as plagiarism. Hodder Education accepts no responsibility for learners plagiarising work from this guide that does or does not meet the assessment criteria.

The sample assignment briefs are provided as a guide to how you might assess the evidence required for all or part of the internal assessment of this Unit. They have not been verified or endorsed by Edexcel and should be internally verified through your own Lead Internal Verifier as with any other assignment briefs, and/or checked through the BTEC assignment checking service.

Orders: please contact Bookpoint Ltd, 130 Milton Park, Abingdon, Oxon OX14 4SB. Telephone: (44) 01235 827720. Fax: (44) 01235 400454. Lines are open from 9.00–5.00, Monday to Saturday, with a 24-hour message answering service. You can also order through our website www.hoddereducation.co.uk

If you have any comments to make about this, or any of our other titles, please send them to educationenquiries@hodder.co.uk

British Library Cataloguing in Publication Data

A catalogue record for this title is available from the British Library

ISBN: 978 1 444 1 86833

Published 2013

Impression number   10 9 8 7 6 5 4 3 2 1

Year   2016 2015 2014 2013

Copyright © 2013 Carole Trotter

Cover photo © Devis Glaokiy – Fotolia

Typeset by Integra Software Services Pvt. Ltd., Pondicherry, India

Printed in Dubai for Hodder Education,
an Hachette UK Company,
338 Euston Road,
London NW1 3BH

Contents

Command words   iv

Introduction   1

Learning aim A: Understand how businesses provide customer service   2

Assessment guidance for learning aim A   16

Learning aim B: Demonstrate appropriate customer service skills in different situations   34

Assessment guidance for learning aim B   40

Sample assignment brief for learning aim A   54

Sample assignment brief for learning aim B   56

Knowledge recap answers   58

Picture credits   60

For attention of the learner

You are not allowed to copy any information from this book and use it as your own evidence. That would count as plagiarism, which is taken very seriously and may result in disqualification. If you are in any doubt at all please speak to your teacher.

Command words

You will find the following command words in the assessment criteria for each unit.

Assess	Give careful consideration to all the factors or events that apply and identify which are the most important or relevant.
Compare	Identify the main factors that apply in two or more situations and explain the similarities and differences or advantages and disadvantages.
Demonstrate	Provide several examples or related evidence which clearly support the arguments you are making. This may include showing practical skills.
Describe	Give a clear description that includes all the relevant features – think of it as painting a picture with words.
Evaluate	Review the information, then bring it together to form a conclusion. Give evidence for each of your views or statements.
Explain	Set out in detail the meaning of something, with reasons. More difficult than describe or list, so it can help to give an example to show what you mean. Start by introducing the topic, then give the 'how' or 'why'.
Justify	Give reasons or evidence to support your opinion or view to show how you arrived at these conclusions.

Introduction

Unit 4: Principles of Customer Service is an internally assessed, optional, specialist unit with two learning aims. This unit focuses on how a business, to remain competitive, must understand the needs and expectations of both internal and external customers. You will need to understand how good communication and interpersonal skills will help deliver and maintain reliable, effective customer service.

This unit will also provide the opportunity for you to demonstrate your customer service skills when working in a customer service role or through participating in appropriate role-play activities.

Each learning aim is divided into main sections. The first section focuses on guidance for the learning aim. All of the topics in the learning aims should be covered in the delivery of the qualification and in this section there are some useful suggestions on what should be covered for each of the topics. When the subheadings in the topics identify an example, these are suggestions for topics, but they can be replaced by more relevant local factors.

The second section provides support with assessment by using evidence generated by a learner, for each grading criterion, with feedback from an assessor. The assessor has highlighted where the evidence is sufficient to satisfy the grading criterion and given developmental feedback when additional work is required.

At the end of the book are examples of assignment briefs for this unit. The unit has been covered by two assignment briefs – the first focuses on learning aim A and the second covers learning aim B. The assignment briefs contain relevant information such as the qualification and unit title, learning aims and grading criteria. The format of the assignment briefs provides room for the assessor to record their name, issue and submission dates and interim review dates. The assignment briefs provide you with clear guidance on the evidence you will need to generate and submit and clearly identify the format in which the evidence should be submitted.

The answers for the knowledge recap questions can be found at the back of this guide.

Learning aim A
Understand how businesses provide customer service

Learning aim A provides the opportunity to get a better understanding of why a business must offer consistent and reliable customer service. Learning aim A also investigates how legislative and regulatory requirements impact on customer service.

Assessment criteria

2A.P1 Describe the different types of customer service provided by two selected businesses.

2A.P2 Describe the characteristics of consistent and reliable customer service.

2A.P3 Explain how organisational procedures and legislation contribute to consistent and reliable customer service.

2A.P4 Explain how legislative and regulatory requirements affect customer service in a selected business.

2A.M1 Compare how two selected businesses satisfy customers.

2A.M2 Explain how a selected business attempts to exceed customer expectations.

2A.M3 Compare the impact of legislative and regulatory requirements affecting customer service on a selected business.

2A.D1 Assess the effect of providing consistent and reliable customer service on the reputation of a selected business.

Topic A.1 The meaning of customer service

Customer service is what a business does to:

a) satisfy the needs
b) meet the expectations of its customers.

Many businesses will have systems in place to ensure that they are meeting the needs of their customers and to make sure that the customers are happy with the service they provide.

Customer service is not just getting the customer to buy the product or service; it is the service the customer gets before, during and after they have purchased the product or service.

Topic A.2 Different customer service roles in a business

A business will employ people in several different job roles and some will have

- roles dealing directly with customers
- roles that do not involve direct customer service.

Roles dealing directly with customers

There are a lot of employees within a business who will be responsible for dealing directly with customers. These include receptionist, contact centre worker, shop assistant and delivery driver.

- The receptionist may be the first person the customer will meet or speak to when contacting or visiting the business. The receptionist will need to create a good impression of the business or the customer may take their custom elsewhere. It will be the receptionist's role to meet and greet all visitors and to respond quickly and professionally to all telephone calls.
- The contact centre worker will not meet the customer face to face but will still need to create a good impression of the company. They will need to be polite and will be required to offer prompt and accurate information to customers.
- The shop assistant will be responsible for supporting the customer while they are buying products or a service. Their role may include providing information or giving advice about the products, or taking payments for products.
- The delivery driver will be responsible for delivering the purchases to the customer's premises and making sure that the customer is happy with the product. The delivery driver should be polite and friendly.

Figure 1.1 Receptionists should create a good impression of the business

Roles that do not involve direct customer service

There are employees within a business who may not have direct contact with the customers but they will still need to create and maintain a good image of the business. These people could be employed as cleaners, gardeners or engineers. A cleaner, gardener or engineer may be required to meet customers or visitors and will need to be polite and helpful.

Topic A.3 The different types of customer service businesses have

There are different ways a business will provide customer service.

Service deliverer

Studied ☐

This will be the member of staff responsible for sales and/or customer service provision. This could be a named salesperson, a customer service assistant or a manager.

Face-to-face customer service

Studied ☐

Most types of businesses have face-to-face customer service.

- **Hotels** – customers will need advice on room availability, meal times, disabled access, laundry service and local places of interest.
- **Restaurants** – customers will want information on menus, wine, vegetarian options and prices.
- **Leisure centres** – customers will want advice on facilities, times and prices.
- **Hospitals** – customers will need advice on how to get to wards or specialist departments, where to find toilets and refreshments, information on car parking and visiting times.
- **Shops** – customers will want information on where to find products, advice on product features, benefits and prices.

Remote customer service

Studied ☐

Some businesses have a call centre and provide support over the phone to customers. More businesses have now email or online support. Some businesses that sell products on a face-to-face basis have remote customer service for their after-sales support.

Customer service teamwork

Studied ☐

Effective customer service requires teamwork and cooperation between the individual employee, the departments and the businesses. All employees should know the procedure for dealing with customer queries and complaints, who to refer the query to and be confident that all queries will be dealt with effectively.

Knowledge recap

1. What customer service provision will be available when visiting a local bus station?
2. What are the benefits when a customer service team work together?

Topic A.4 Customer satisfaction

What is customer satisfaction?

Studied ☐

Customer satisfaction is when customers are happy and satisfied with:

a) the product or service they have purchased
b) the service they received when making the purchase
c) the after-sales service.

A business will need to know what the customers want and expect and then provide this. The business will need to ensure that:

- **Customers are confident with the service provided.** A customer will want to be sure that the service they have been provided with is accurate and honest. A customer will not return to a business if they find out the information they have been given is wrong or inaccurate.
- **The product or service is value for money.** A customer will want to know that they have purchased goods or services that are value for money. They will not be satisfied if they find out they could have bought the same product or service more cheaply from a competitor.

A customer who is satisfied with the service they have received will:

- **Return to purchase other products.** This will increase sales for the business.
- **Tell others about the business and the products or service it sells.** This will enhance the reputation of the business and could result in more sales.
- **Become loyal to the business.** A customer who is happy and satisfied will return to the business to purchase from a different range of products or services. For example, if a customer is happy with their new furniture, they will return to the shop when looking for carpets.

Different ways businesses can satisfy customers

Studied ☐

There are several different ways a business can satisfy customers. These include:

- **Providing a good quality product or service.** Providing good quality products that do not break down on a regular basis is important to customer satisfaction. If customers have to return products which are faulty or if the service they require is not efficient, they will be unsatisfied.

- **Providing extra services (for example delivery and after-sales care).** Customers will not want to have to make their own arrangements for delivery of large items or pay additional delivery costs. A customer would not be happy if they found out that competitors provided free delivery. After purchasing the product, the customer will want to be able to contact the business easily for additional information or guidance, for maintenance or to update their product.
- **Providing a reliable and speedy service.** The customer will want to be served quickly and efficiently. For example, the customer will not want to wait while the salesperson finishes gossiping with a colleague. When a customer has decided to purchase a product they will not want to be informed that they will need to wait for new stock to come in or that there is a six-week wait for delivery.
- **Providing value for money.** A customer will want to know that the product they have purchased is good value for the money that they paid. The customer will not be happy if they find cheaper products with the same benefits and features.
- **Providing information and advice.** A salesperson should be able to provide the customer with advice and guidance that is accurate.

Figure 1.2 Providing accurate advice and guidance increases customer satisfaction

- **Providing support with problems.** Any problems or complaints should be dealt with efficiently. The business should have clear procedures in place for dealing with customers' problems and complaints.

Knowledge recap

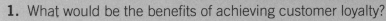

1. What would be the benefits of achieving customer loyalty?
2. What could a local bus station introduce to achieve customer satisfaction?

Topic A.5 Different ways that businesses can provide consistent and reliable customer service

There are several different ways a business can provide a consistent and reliable service for its customers.

Staff knowledge of the job role and products and services

Studied ☐

Staff should be able to fulfil their job role. For example, someone employed in technical support should be able to talk a customer through the steps needed to overcome a technical problem in a clear, concise and patient manner. Staff should have knowledge about the range of products or services they sell and be able to explain their features to customers – this may involve being able to demonstrate how a product works.

Staff attitude and behaviour

Studied ☐

Sufficient staff should be available to support the customer with purchasing products or services. Customers should be served politely, promptly and efficiently.

Figure 1.3 Staff should always be polite when serving customers

Meeting specific customer needs

Studied ☐

Some customers, for example those with young children or those in wheelchairs, may require additional help when purchasing or packing products. Staff should be trained in how to support customers with hearing or sight problems and should be aware that some customers may have problems in communicating or understanding because of language barriers.

Working under pressure

Studied ☐

A business will have busy periods when employees will be working under pressure, but the business must ensure that support and help are available. Employees will need to know where to go for support and advice. Employees who are working under pressure must try to remain calm and must always be polite.

Confirming service meets needs and expectations

Studied ☐

The employee should be talking and listening to the customer to establish whether they were happy and satisfied with the service provided. A business could introduce customer satisfaction surveys or questionnaires to identify areas of customer service that could be improved.

Dealing with problems

Studied ☐

The business must implement clear procedures for dealing with customers' queries or complaints. Any complaint should be logged and dealt with quickly and efficiently.

Figure 1.4 Employees should know what to do when a customer complains

Knowledge recap

1. What could a business do to ensure that staff demonstrate the right attitude and behaviour?

2. How would a business evaluate its customer service provision?

Topic A.6 The effect of good customer service on the reputation of a business

To be successful, it is important for a business to achieve and be recognised for providing customers with good customer service.

Building a good reputation

Studied ☐

A good reputation is important to the success and survival of the business. Customers will trade with a business that has a good reputation and this will increase sales and profits.

A good reputation can be damaged by comments passed on by customers about poor quality products or bad customer service. The reputation of a business can also be damaged by comments made by employees who are not happy in their job role. Customers will not want to deal with a business that has a bad reputation or one that has received bad coverage in the media and this will affect sales figures and profits and could affect the survival of a business.

To build and achieve a good reputation a business will need to:

- **Sell quality products or services.** A business must not sell goods that are faulty or poor quality.
- **Sell products or services that are value for money.** To maintain sales and market share a business will need to monitor its prices and products against those offered by its competitors to ensure that it offers its customers value for money.
- **Be consistent in the service and products it offers.** A business must check that it is providing good quality products. Customers will expect a consistently high level of customer service, so it is important that all employees are trained to give effective customer service.
- **Be reliable.** A customer will need to know that they can rely on the business to provide good quality products which are reliable and do what they are supposed to do.
- **Provide a trustworthy service.** A business must provide honest and reliable information about the products and services available. If a customer feels that they have been cheated or misled, they will move their custom elsewhere.

Effects of building a good reputation

A business that does achieve and establish a good reputation will experience:

- **Increased sales** – customers will buy from a business that has established a good reputation.
- **Increased profit** – increased sales will increase business profits.

Figure 1.5 Increased sales and profit will result from having a good reputation

- **Retention of existing customers** – customers will return to a business where they have found good quality products and reliable customer service.
- **New customers** – customers will find out about a business before they shop there. A business that has received positive media coverage will entice new customers to shop there.
- **Word-of-mouth recommendation** – customers will be willing to recommend to family, friends and colleagues a business that has provided them with quality products and good customer service.
- **Competitive advantage** – customers would rather shop and deal with a business with a good reputation than use its competitors.
- **Staff job satisfaction and motivation** – employees and potential employees would prefer to work for a company that has established a good reputation. If the managers are working towards achieving constantly high standards, then employees will also be motivated to maintain those standards. All employees will achieve job satisfaction if customers are content and applaud the service they provide.

Knowledge recap

1. How could a business establish a good reputation?
2. What would be the benefits of establishing a good reputation?

Topic A.7 Different ways of exceeding customer expectations

A business can introduce several different measures to ensure it exceeds the expectations of its customers.

Providing value for money

`Studied ▢`

Customers will return to the business if they feel the products or service were value for the money they paid.

Providing information and advice quickly

`Studied ▢`

Customers should be provided with all the relevant information and instructions on the products or services they purchase. Customers may need written or verbal instructions for assembling or using a product and these should be available at the time of sale. Where possible, staff should be able to demonstrate how a product works. Advice and support should be accurate and provided promptly to customers.

Providing additional help and assistance

`Studied ▢`

A business will be recognised and remembered by customers if it provides additional help and assistance. This could include:

- **Dealing promptly with problems**
- **Offering discounts** – customers will compare prices between competitors and will look around for products or services with special offers and discounts.

Figure 1.6 Discounts can be offered to attract customers

- **Offering additional products or services** – customers will compare what added value businesses are offering with a product or service. For the added value to appeal more than its competitors, the business will need to do its research to find out what customers want.
- **Providing information on returns policy** – a business should have a clearly defined returns policy that all employees are aware of and this should be communicated to customers.

Providing help and assistance for customers with special requirements

The business is responsible for providing exceptional help and assistance for customers with special requirements. For example, a customer in a wheelchair or with young children in a pushchair may need additional help and support when browsing and paying for their purchases. By offering support that the customer had not expected, the business will create a lasting impression of looking after its customers.

Figure 1.7 Businesses should provide assistance for customers with special requirements

Knowledge recap

1. How could a travel agent exceed customer expectations?

2. What support could a business provide for customers with sight problems?

Topic A.8 Providing effective customer service through organisational procedures

Providing effective customer service

Studied ☐

There are several ways a business can provide effective customer service. These include the following:

- **Monitoring customer service** – this could be achieved by talking and listening to customers, carrying out customer surveys and reviewing the type of complaints made by customers.

Figure 1.8 Customer surveys are an effective way of monitoring customer service

- **Following codes of practice introduced by the industry, profession, organisation or business** – businesses could belong to an industry association, for example ABTA for travel agents, and this will reassure customers that they are dealing with a reputable business.
- **Meeting legal and regulatory requirements** – a business will need to be aware of any changes to legislation and take any relevant action.
- **Having ethical standards** – a business will need to ensure that the products or services it offers do not offend any existing or potential customers, for example selling products which have been tested on animals or products that are not environmentally friendly.

The business will achieve this by:

Ensuring that correct procedures are introduced and abided by – to achieve this, the business should have clear policies and procedures in place for the following:

- when to refer problems to a line manager
- dealing with refunds
- who an employee can contact for guidance and advice
- treating all customers equally.

Minimising hazards and risks – this will include:

- identifying where customers could be injured
- informing people of dangers, for example signs identifying wet floors
- complying with fire regulations, including clear exit signs, fire extinguishers correctly located, training for employees on fire drills, regular fire and evacuation drills, set meeting points
- clear procedures for dealing with security alerts, including evacuation procedures, meeting points and checking that all employees have been accounted for.

The purpose of organisational procedures

Studied ☐

Businesses should implement organisational procedures that contribute to consistent and reliable customer service. This will be achieved by:

- providing customers with a service that exceeds the customer service offered by competitors. Offering a more efficient and effective customer service will give the business the opportunity to gain a competitive edge and improve its market share.
- ensuring that the company mission or vision statements are followed. The mission statement will inform both employees and customers what the business does and what its objectives are.
- ensuring external quality benchmarks are met. A business must check and regularly review that its products or services satisfy the quality benchmarks demanded by the industry.

✓

Knowledge recap

1. Why is it important for a business to minimise risks and hazards?

2. What is a mission statement?

Topic A.9 Complying with legislative and regulatory customer service requirements

All businesses must introduce and implement policies and procedures that meet and satisfy legal and regulatory requirements.

The Sale of Goods Act (1994)

Studied ▢

This states that goods must fit the description given; the goods must be fit for purpose; the goods must be of a satisfactory quality. When products or services are not fit for purpose or are of poor quality, the business is legally obliged to resolve the issues.

The Safety, Health and Welfare at Work Act (2005)

Studied ▢

This states that the employer must provide a safe and secure workplace for both employees and customers. The employer must provide employees with all the necessary equipment and protective clothing and training. The employees must use the equipment safely and wear the protective clothing provided.

The Data Protection Act (1998)

Studied ▢

This was introduced to protect personal information stored on computers or in paper-based files. The act does not prevent a business from having personal information but does highlight what can and cannot be done with this information.

The Equal Opportunities Act (2006) and the more recent Equality Act of 2010

Studied ▢

These were introduced so that everyone could be treated fairly in the workplace. This includes fair treatment when applying for a job, at work and for promotion opportunities. The Equality Act 2010 also protects people from discrimination when they access goods, facilities and services.

Knowledge recap

1. List three employer responsibilities from the Safety, Health and Welfare at Work Act.
2. Why was the Data Protection Act needed?

Learning aim A: Understand how businesses provide customer service

Assessment guidance for learning aim A

2A.P1 Describe the different types of customer service provided by two selected businesses

✍ **Learner answer**

> The businesses I have chosen to use for this are the Co-op Travel Agency and The Rink, a local leisure centre.

Assessor report: The command verb here is describe. To achieve this, the learner will need to give a clear description of the types of customer service provided by the two businesses, including all the relevant features.

The learner has made a good choice by selecting to provide evidence on two different types of businesses for 2A.P1.

> The Co-op is responsible for supporting customers in planning and booking their holidays. The Co-op has staff who are trained to offer advice on travel, holidays in the UK and abroad. The staff will help with booking flights, hotels and car hire. If customers are not sure what they want there are lots of brochures to look through or to take away.
>
> Customers will spend a lot of time in the shop so the Co-op provides seats for the customers to use and if it takes a long time to find the right holiday the customers are offered hot drinks.
>
> The staff will provide customers with information about the places they are going and will give them information sheets on travelling abroad. The information sheets provide a checklist for what to take and information about keeping safe and healthy while on holiday.

Assessor report: The learner has provided a good description of the customer service provided by the Co-op and could just add a little more information about how the Co-op deals with customer queries or complaints. The learner will then need to describe the customer service provided by their second business.

The Co-op deals with customers face to face and by telephone and email. The staff are smart and friendly and will try to help solve any problems. They do offer additional advice about insurance, passports and visas.

They offer prices which are similar to other travel agents but sometimes they have special discounts or offers. There are loyalty cards for customers who shop there regularly.

The manager is usually in the shop and will help customers who have complaints or problems. At busy times the staff will still focus on finding the right holiday even though other customers are waiting.

Assessor report: The learner has submitted sufficient evidence for the Co-op but still needs to describe the customer service for their second business before 2A.P1 can be awarded.

The Rink is a large leisure centre where there is a gym, a swimming pool and a large ice rink [a]. The Rink is open to all age groups and there are shower, toilet and café facilities around the building.

Assessor report: The learner has listed the facilities available at The Rink [a] but to achieve 2A.P1 will need to describe the different types of customer service provided.

Assessor report – overall

Is the evidence sufficient to satisfy the grading criterion?

The learner has produced some good work for the Co-op and has started to provide some evidence for their second business.

The learner has not yet produced sufficient evidence for 2A.P1 because they have only listed the facilities available at The Rink [a] and have not described the types of customer service they provide. The learner could describe the customer service provided at reception, when using the leisure facilities and in the rest areas such as the café.

What additional evidence, if any, is required?

To achieve 2A.P1 the learner will need to provide information on the types of customer service provided by The Rink.

2A.P2 Describe the characteristics of consistent and reliable customer service

✍ Learner answer

Good customer service is when the customers are happy with the service from employees and the products they have bought are good value for money. The service would have to be consistently good and not just for regular customers or customers who spend a lot of money. Consistent and reliable customer service is:

- staff knowing about the products and providing information
- staff being polite and getting to know customers
- staff serving customers quickly
- staff helping customers with packing
- staff looking clean and smart.

The first point is that staff should know about the products they sell. Staff should be able to explain the features and benefits of having the product to the customer. They will be able to answer customers' questions and give them advice.

Assessor report: The command verb for 2A.P2 is **describe**. To achieve this the learner will need to give a clear description that includes all the relevant features.

The learner has made a good start by stating what good customer service is and listing the characteristics of good customer service. The learner has described the first point in their list and to achieve 2A.P2 will need to do the same for all the other listed points.

Assessor report – overall

Is the evidence sufficient to satisfy the grading criterion?

The learner has clearly identified what represents consistent and reliable customer service. The learner has developed this by listing the characteristics and describing one point from the list. To achieve 2A.P2 the learner will now need to continue and describe all the points listed.

What additional evidence, if any, is required?

To achieve 2A.P2 the learner will need to describe all the characteristics listed.

Explain how organisational procedures and legislation contribute to consistent and reliable customer service

✍ Learner answer

For a business to have good customer service they must have procedures in place so staff know what they are expected to do. A business will also need to make sure that they are not breaking any laws such as the Safety, Health and Welfare at Work Act, Data Protection Act, Equal Opportunities Act and especially the Sale of Goods Act. A business will not want to be known for breaking the law because this may mean that customers will go somewhere else to buy their products or services.

Assessor report: The command verb for 2A.P3 is **explain**. To achieve this, the learner will need to set out in detail, with reasons, how organisational procedures and legislation contribute to consistent and reliable customer service. Explaining is more difficult than describing or listing, so it can help to give an example to show what you mean. Start by introducing the topic, then give the 'how' or 'why'.

The first paragraph highlights that the learner understands what is required for this grading criterion.

For a business to offer a good customer service the staff must have an understanding of all the policies and procedures and the laws that protect them and the customers.

The business will need to have a written procedure on how to deal with customers' questions, queries and complaints. The procedures are there so that employees know what they must do if a customer has a query or complaint. The procedure will mean that all the customers are treated the same and staff will know when they are required to pass problems on to a manager. If the procedures are clear it means that customers' problems can be dealt with quickly. If staff do not know what the procedure is, the customers may be given the wrong information. This will make customers angry and annoyed and they may decide to go to the competitors.

The staff will need to know about the policy for returning goods which are broken or faulty. The business may have a policy that only managers can offer refunds or exchange goods, but if the staff do not know this they may give a refund or an exchange. This may mean that some customers get a refund when others will not and they will not be happy.

Assessor report: The learner has clearly explained why a business needs to have procedures and now needs to explain how legislation contributes to consistent and reliable customer service.

Some laws are very important and make sure that the business provides a good service for the customers.

A business must sell products that do what they say and they must be working. This is in the Sale of Goods Act, which also says that a business must replace goods if they do not do the things they should. It is important that a business sells goods that are a good quality or the customers will not come back and will shop with the competitors. If the business sells goods which are faulty they are not providing a good customer service and they will get a bad reputation. If the customers are not happy or do not trust the business they will go to competitors. This means that they will lose sales and then profits.

The Safety, Health and Welfare at Work Act says that an employer must provide a safe place for customers and staff. The business must check that their building is safe and there are no hazards which could hurt or injure staff or customers. A business is not providing a good customer service if customers slip on wet floors or trip on loose carpets or wires. Customers will want to be safe so will use businesses that look clean and tidy and where they can easily get to the products they want to buy.

The Data Protection Act protects the personal details of staff (a) and these cannot be passed on. The Data Protection Act will mean that all the information about the staff's name, address, telephone numbers is safe and secure.

The Equal Opportunities Act is so that all staff have to be treated the same and no one can have special treatment. A business must pay staff the same for doing the same job. When staff are treated the same they will want to do their job well and this will mean that customers get a good customer service. If staff feel they are treated differently this will affect the service they give to the customers. The business must treat all customers fairly and equally. Customers would be annoyed if they found out that some customers were being given special treatment (b).

Assessor report: The learner has explained how legislation will help provide consistent and reliable customer service. The learner must identify that the Data Protection Act [a] will also protect personal details for customers. The learner could have used an example to explain discrimination of customers [b].

Assessor report – overall

Is the evidence sufficient to satisfy the grading criterion?

The learner has produced some good evidence and explained why workplace procedures play an important part in a business, providing consistent and reliable customer service. The last section does make reference to all the legislation listed in the unit specification, but to achieve 2A.P3 the learner must correct the information for the Data Protection Act [a].

What additional evidence, if any, is required?

To achieve 2A.P3 the learner will need to clearly highlight that the Data Protection Act was introduced to protect customers as well as employees.

2A.P4 Explain how legislative and regulatory requirements affect customer service in a selected business

✍ Learner answer

Legislation and regulatory requirements will affect customer service in all businesses but I have chosen to write about The Rink because it is a business I know well.

Assessor report: The command verb for 2A.P4 is **explain**. To achieve this, the learner will need to set out in detail, with reasons, how legislative and regulatory requirements affect customer service in their chosen business.

The learner has identified their selected business and has correctly chosen to focus on a business they know well.

There is health and safety legislation that says that The Rink needs to make sure that the premises, fixtures and equipment are safe for people to use and these have to be checked to make sure they meet regulations. Customers would prefer to use premises that have been checked and that are safe. The equipment needs to be safe to satisfy health and safety legislation and The Rink is keen to implement anything that keeps their customers safe and that will prevent accidents. It would be bad for the reputation of The Rink if customers were injured when using the gym or other facilities.

The Rink is responsible for disposing of rubbish and waste regularly and safely but customers would not use The Rink if it smelt bad. The regulations are there but The Rink wants to provide a clean, safe place so that customers will want to come and use the facilities.

The Rink is responsible to check that the goods they sell are good value and will do what they should [a]. Customers can buy lots of items at The Rink like arm bands and goggles for swimming. Customers will not come back to the centre if the goods they buy do not work properly and if they get injured they may take The Rink to court. Any bad publicity will mean that The Rink will lose customers and sales.

Assessor report: The learner has explained how health and safety legislation and regulations contribute to consistent and reliable customer service. The learner has also briefly made reference to the sale of goods [a] and now needs to provide evidence for other regulations and legislation.

The Rink is responsible for ensuring that customers have a health check and a full induction to the facilities, especially in the gym. The Rink follows regulations because they want to protect their customers from accidents or getting injured.

The Rink only employs people who have the right qualifications and training to do the job and job adverts state that The Rink is an equal opportunities employer. To be a trainer the staff must have the right qualification and first-aid training. Everyone gets on well and are treated the same. Any member of staff can apply for promotion or any new job [a]. The Rink displays all the staff qualifications and this will help customers feel confident in the trainers' skills.

All customers are treated fairly and equally. All customers are provided with information about the facilities and are encouraged to try new things. Childcare facilities are provided so mums and dads can use the facilities and support is available for customers with disabilities. There are women-only swimming sessions.

Assessor report: The learner has explained how their selected business looks after customers by following regulations to ensure they are fit and able to use the facilities. The learner has briefly made reference to the Equal Opportunities Act [a]. To achieve 2A.P4 the learner must include some information about the Data Protection Act.

Assessor report – overall

Is the evidence sufficient to satisfy the grading criterion?

The learner has produced some good evidence and explained how some legislative and regulatory requirements affect the customer service in their chosen business. To achieve 2A.P4 the learner must add a short paragraph on how data protection contributes to consistent and reliable customer service. Customers' and employees' records will have a lot of personal information and it is important that they know this information will not be released to other organisations. Customers will be providing information about their health and medication and will not want The Rink to pass on this information.

What additional evidence, if any, is required?

To achieve 2A.P4 the learner will need to explain how data protection contributes to consistent and reliable customer service.

Compare how two selected businesses satisfy customers

✎ **Learner answer**

The businesses I have chosen to use for 2A.M1 are the Co-op Travel Agency and The Rink, a local leisure centre.

Assessor report: The command verb for this assessment criterion is compare. The learner will need to identify how their two selected businesses satisfy customers and explain the similarities and differences in how they achieve this.

The learner has set the scene by identifying which businesses they will use and has chosen to use businesses which operate in different markets. It is beneficial for learners to use the same businesses from 2A.P1 and develop the evidence they have produced for this grading criterion.

The table identifies what Co-op Travel and The Rink have in place for customers.

	Co-op Travel	The Rink
Sales staff	Sufficient staff on weekdays but not sufficient extra staff for weekends All trained and qualified	Sufficient staff to supervise the classes Qualified trainers and keep-fit instructors
Customer service desk	No – managers deal with customer complaints	No – but a named person responsible for customer service management
Dealing with problems	Not always prompt	Quick but not consistent
Products	Holidays, flights, hotels, car hire, airport parking	Ice rink, swimming pool, gym, fitness classes
Value for money	Provides special offers and will match competitor prices	Less expensive than the closest competitor, which is 10 miles away. Does have some special offers
Loyal customers	Some who book holidays each year – loyalty cards	Customers who regularly use the centre
Extra customer service facilities	Chairs, selection of brochures, information on resorts, insurance Refreshments at times	Showers, toilets and cafés, trainers and keep-fit instructors who give advice on fitness and health
Support for customers with special needs	Good access for all customers	Access to all facilities but access to café is a struggle for wheelchairs Special keep-fit classes for the elderly and women-only swimming mornings
Providing information	Accurate but customers may have to wait	Accurate and prompt

Assessor report: The learner has produced a very detailed table which describes the services available for customers at each business. The learner will now need to compare the points they have described.

The Co-op has sufficient staff to book holidays and answer customer queries during the week, but at weekends, the busiest time, there are often very few extra staff available. It takes a long time to select the right holiday and other customers have to wait, stand around or look at brochures until a member of staff is free. The Rink is different and has a lot of staff on duty and always has sufficient staff to supervise the gym, swimming pool and any special classes. It has never happened yet but the classes would have to be cancelled, because of safety reasons, if there were insufficient trained staff.

Both the Co-op and The Rink have staff who are trained and have the right qualifications to do their jobs.

Assessor report: The learner has started to compare by identifying the similarity in having staff that are trained and qualified and the differences in staff availability. The learner will now need to apply this to the other points listed in the table.

The Co-op and The Rink provide all the relevant facilities for their customers and they both provide discounts and special offers. The Rink has loyal customers who will visit the centre daily or regularly and the Co-op does have some loyal customers who book their yearly holiday with them. The Co-op customers do have a loyalty card and will get vouchers and this is something The Rink could do.

They both provide customers with accurate advice and information but at times the Co-op customers may have to wait until the next working day to get the information.

There are extra facilities available for customers at both the Co-op and The Rink and they both have facilities for customers with disabilities or who have special requirements.

Assessor report: The learner has continued to compare how the businesses satisfy customers, but to achieve 2A.M1 the learner must compare how the businesses deal with complaints or problems – an important element in satisfying customer needs.

Assessor report – overall

Is the evidence sufficient to satisfy the grading criterion?

The learner has started to produce some good work and is correctly focusing the evidence on the businesses that were used in 2A.P1. The table describes all of the relevant points in satisfying customer needs, but the learner has not compared one important element – how the businesses deal with complaints and problems.

What additional evidence, if any, is required?

To achieve 2A.M1 the learner will need to compare how the two businesses deal with customer complaints and problems.

2A.M2 Explain how a selected business attempts to exceed customer expectations

✎ Learner answer

The business I am going to use is the Co-op Travel Agency.

Assessor report: The command verb for 2A.M2 is <u>explain</u>. To achieve this, the learner will need to set out in detail how their chosen business attempts to exceed customer expectations.

The learner has currently identified the business they will use for this grading criterion. It is important that a learner chooses to write about a business they know well.

The points I am going to write about are:

- providing value for money
- giving advice and information
- additional help and assistance
- dealing promptly with problems
- discounts and special offers
- extra products
- support for customers with special requirements
- satisfaction questionnaires.

Customers spend a lot of their pay on a holiday so will want the travel agents to be efficient and help them find a suitable holiday. The customer tells the staff what type of holiday they want, where and when, and then the staff spend time finding an appropriate holiday. The Co-op staff will look through brochures to find the best deals for holidays and will look at holidays with different companies to find one which matches what the customer wants. Sometimes they will suggest flights with one company and a hotel from another because it is better value for money. At times there are special deals such as free holidays for children or discounts if you book early. The Co-op will sometimes have special offers such as free in-flight meals, free insurance, extra luggage allowance, online check-in, online booking for seats on the flight. Some of the special offers may appeal more to one customer than another but are often similar to other travel agents. One thing that competitors do not have is a loyalty card that gives points for the money spent. Later in the year the points become vouchers which the customers can use to pay for, or in part payment for, shopping.

The staff will provide additional information on, and if required will book, car parking, insurance, car hire, tickets for special events or places of interest. Additional advice is also given on passports, visas, what to pack, what you can or cannot take on the plane and the weather abroad.

Assessor report: The learner has listed all the relevant points and has begun to explain how the business attempts to exceed customer expectations. The learner has explained how the Co-op provides additional information and advice and how it provides value for money.

If the staff do not know the answers to some questions they will find the information and forward it on; at times a response may not be possible until a department reopens on Monday morning. If there is a problem with the holiday or some parts need to be changed the Co-op will provide prompt guidance so that the customer does not incur extra charges or lose the holiday. Customers are asked to complete a questionnaire which provides feedback for the Co-op on what the customers thought about the service provided and how they felt it could be improved.

Assessor report: The learner has continued to explain the points from their list but has not provided evidence for one important point for 2A.M2: how the Co-op supports customers with special requirements.

Assessor report – overall

Is the evidence sufficient to satisfy the grading criterion?

The learner has explained most of the relevant points but has not provided any evidence on how the business supports customers with special requirements. The learner has correctly identified this important point in the list but has made no further reference to it.

What additional evidence, if any, is required?

To achieve 2A.M2 the learner will need to add a paragraph on how the Co-op provides exceptional help and assistance for customers with special requirements.

Compare the impact of legislative and regulatory requirements affecting customer service on a selected business

✍ Learner answer

The business I have chosen to use for 2A.M3 is The Rink, which is a local leisure centre.

Assessor report: The command verb for this criterion is **compare**. The learner will need to identify the similarities and differences between how the legislative and regulatory requirements affecting customer service impact on a business.

The learner has set the scene by identifying which business they will use.

I have used a table to list the main points covered by the legislative and regulatory requirements.

Health and Safety	Data Protection	Sale of Goods	Equal Opportunity
Protects customers and employees	Protects customers and employees	Protects customers and employees	Protects customers and employees
Provide a safe workplace	Information must be kept securely and must be accurate	Sells goods or services which are fit for purpose, safe and work properly	Treating everyone fairly
Keep staff and customers safe	Remove old information	Goods must do what they say and be good quality	Providing access to facilities for all customers
Guidance on using equipment	Not pass on information unless given permission	Must solve any problems	Providing equal opportunities for employment and promotion
Provide staff training and any necessary equipment	Only have the information they need		
Safe storage and handling of substances			
Risk assessment to identify hazards			

Assessor report: The learner has currently just listed the main points of the legislative and regulatory requirements and now, to satisfy the requirements of 2A.M3, will need to compare them.

There are posters all around The Rink which provide information on health and safety and posters in the shop, café and reception about the centre policy for the goods they sell; what to do if goods are faulty and their refund policy. Customers are well informed about health and safety and what to do if they are not happy with what they buy. There is information in the centre leaflets about the facilities and support they provide for people with disabilities and keeping safe and healthy while using the centre.

Assessor report: The learner has highlighted similarities and differences on where The Rink displays or provides legislative and regulatory information for customers. The learner now needs to focus on the facilities and support at the centre.

Customers will want to feel safe when they are at The Rink and it is the responsibility of The Rink under the health and safety law to make sure that this happens. For customers to use the equipment safely they will need guidance and support from qualified trainers. To do this The Rink will need to employ people with the right experience and qualifications and this will mean not discriminating against potential employees who have these. Customers will come to the centre if they have trust in the skills of the people who are supporting them and keeping them safe in the pool, on the ice and in the gym. So both the health and safety and the equal opportunities legislation will help to keep customers safe.

Assessor report: The learner has compared how parts of both the health and safety and equal opportunities legislative and regulatory requirements help The Rink keep customers safe. The learner also needs to provide evidence for data protection and sale of goods.

Customers will purchase items from the centre and the Sale of Goods Act states that goods must be fit for purpose. The Safety, Health and Welfare at Work Act also looks at keeping employees and customers safe. If the centre sold items which were not good quality for use in the gym, pool and on the ice there could be accidents and customers could get injured. An example is, if a customer bought arm bands at the centre to use in the pool and if the arm bands did not stay inflated this could put the customer in danger and pool staff could also be injured trying to help the customer. So both the sale of goods and health and safety are similar because they are there to protect customers and employees. The Rink does check that products are good quality and not faulty before they are placed on display and this should prevent injuries and accidents. If someone did get injured all staff are trained in first aid and know the drill for emergencies.

The Rink does employ maintenance staff to keep everything working as required by the health and safety legislation. All customers, including wheelchair users, people with disabilities such as sight or hearing problems, families with children and babies, non-English-speaking customers, are treated fairly and have access to the building and the equipment. The Rink is moving the access to the café which is a problem for customers in wheelchairs; the access is satisfactory for health and safety but not satisfactory for equal opportunities.

Assessor report: The learner has compared how parts of the health and safety, equal opportunities and sale of goods legislative and regulatory requirements impact on customer service at The Rink. The learner has listed information about data protection in the table but has not provided any further information.

Assessor report – overall

Is the evidence sufficient to satisfy the grading criterion?

The learner has compared how health and safety, equal opportunities and sale of goods impact on customer service, but not data protection. The learner could comment, for example, that data is needed and recorded for equal opportunities purposes but must, to satisfy data protection, be kept secure.

What additional evidence, if any, is required?

To achieve 2A.M3 the learner will need to compare how the impact of data protection is similar to or different from the other legislative and regulatory requirements and the extent each impact is likely to have on the selected business.

2A.D1 Assess the effect of providing consistent and reliable customer service on the reputation of a selected business

✍ **Learner answer**

The business I will use to provide the evidence for 2A.D1 is Co-op Travel who provide consistent and reliable customer service.

- products which are value for money
- staff knowledge of holiday destinations and places to visit
- qualified staff to advise customers
- support from managers and colleagues during busy times
- added value – different than competitors
- dealing quickly with problems or complaints
- customer surveys and review of service provided.

Assessor report: The command verb here is **assess**. The learner will need to give careful consideration to all the factors and events that apply and identify which are the most important or relevant.

The learner has identified and listed how the Co-op provides consistent and reliable service and will now need to use these points to assess their effect on the Co-op's reputation.

The Co-op Travel is the largest independent travel agent and it must follow the guidelines set down by ABTA and ATOL. It has some strong competition from companies such as Thomson, Hayes, Thomas Cook and from airlines such as easyJet. Customers will save their money to spend on a holiday so they will want value for money and will shop around for good deals. Very few customers who come into the Co-op will know what they want to purchase so will need the guidance of experienced and qualified staff. The Co-op staff are well qualified and do provide a very good service which will make customers return year after year, helping improve sales and profits. Customers will appreciate and remember any additional information given by the staff which helped them. People always talk about their holidays and this could help persuade new customers to use the Co-op meaning more sales and profits.

Assessor report: The learner has briefly assessed how the qualified staff at the Co-op will encourage customers to return each year and how word-of-mouth recommendations could boost sales and profits.

To achieve 2A.D1 the learner will need to assess how the other listed points have an effect on the Co-op's reputation.

If customers discovered that the information was not accurate they would lose trust in the Co-op and go elsewhere. If customers are unhappy with the service, information or advice they will tell their friends, family and colleagues and this will affect the Co-op's reputation and their sales and profits. People always talk more about things that went wrong than things that are okay.

The Co-op, like most travel agents, gets busy during dinner hours and at weekends. Customers will want time to discuss holidays but will want to be served quickly. At busy times customers are kept waiting and although managers and office staff do help, there are not sufficient computers to make bookings. The staff do apologise, but customers may leave without booking and this could affect sales, profits and their reputation.

The Co-op sells holidays which are similar to their competitors and so will need to use different offers and added extras so that their packages appeal more. The Co-op will use the added extras to attract new customers and to retain existing customers and this will protect or maybe increase sales and profits.

The Co-op uses questionnaires to find out if their customers are happy with the service they provide. The outcome from the surveys is fed back to staff and if problems are identified the manager is told what must be done to improve the service.

Assessor report: The learner has continued to assess how relevant points will affect the Co-op's reputation. The learner has not provided any evidence on how the Co-op deals with problems and complaints.

Assessor report – overall

Is the evidence sufficient to satisfy the grading criterion?

The learner has assessed most of the relevant points but has not provided any evidence on how the Co-op deals with problems or complaints. This is important because customers talk about problems and complaints and this could affect the Co-op's reputation.

What additional evidence, if any, is required?

To achieve 2A.D1 the learner will need to assess how the process used to deal with problems and complaints could affect the reputation of the Co-op.

Learning aim B

Demonstrate appropriate customer service skills in different situations

Learning aim B provides the opportunity to learn about the different types of customers and the skills required to deliver efficient and effective customer service.

Assessment criteria

2B.P5 Describe how a selected business meets the needs and expectations of three different types of customer.

2B.P6 Describe, using examples, the limits of authority that would apply when delivering customer service.

2B.P7 Demonstrate effective communication skills to meet customer needs when dealing with three different customer types in customer service situations.

2B.M4 Demonstrate effective communication skills when responding to customer problems and complaints in three customer service situations.

2B.D2 Evaluate the effectiveness of own customer service skills, justifying areas for improvement.

Topic B.1 Customers

Types of customer

Studied ☐

- **Internal customers** can be anyone employed in the organisation or business. They could be a manager, a line manager or supervisor, a secretary or receptionist, someone in a different department or at a different branch, or a colleague. Internal customers could also be owners or shareholders.
- **External customers** are customers who are not directly linked to the business. External customers can be existing customers or new customers. They can be an individual customer or a group of customers such as a club, or another business.
- **Customers with special requirements** are customers who may require additional support when accessing the premises and purchasing goods or services. These could include customers who are non-English speaking, elderly customers, parents with young children, customers with special needs such as limited mobility, or who require hearing or visual support.

Differences between internal and external customers

Internal customers are people who are employed by the business. External customers have no connection with the business, they just want to purchase goods or a service.

The internal customers will know the business well and will be familiar with the person selling the product or service. If a business provides a poor service for its internal customers, this could impact on the service or products provided for external customers. For example, if a receptionist is provided with inaccurate information about sales, they could pass on this information to external customers and the external customers will not be happy. An internal customer is still a customer and needs to be treated with the same respect and professionalism, even though they may be getting a product or service more cheaply. If this does not happen, this can create a negative attitude among staff which will pass on to external customers.

Factors that impact on different customer service expectations

- **Age of customers** – for example, an elderly customer may want more time or support in making a decision. A young person may want information on the latest mobile phones.
- **Culture** – knowledge of different cultures could prevent any misunderstandings.
- **Image of the business** – creating the right image is essential to the success of the business. If a customer likes what they hear and see about the business, they will use it.
- **Public image of the owner** – the owner of the business must maintain an excellent professional public image. If the owner receives any adverse or bad publicity it will have an impact on the image of the business and may affect sales.
- **Disposable income** – all customers expect to be treated equally, whether they can only afford an imitation or they can afford to buy the real thing. Customers with large disposable incomes and money to spend may want a more personal service.

Knowledge recap

1. Why is it important for a business to have a positive image?
2. Who are customers with special requirements?

Topic B.2 Skills required to deliver consistent and reliable customer service

There are several skills needed to provide excellent customer service.

Being professional and creating a good impression

`Studied ☐`

- Display good manners – be polite and helpful
- Be appropriately dressed – look clean and smart
- Use appropriate language – do not use jargon
- Have good posture/body language – maintain positive body language that demonstrates that you are listening to the customer
- Maintain a tidy work area – a clean, organised work area

Having a positive attitude

`Studied ☐`

- Good timekeeping – arriving on time for work
- Being conscientious – careful and hard working
- Being motivated – enthusiastic about doing a good job

Effective communication with customers

`Studied ☐`

- Verbal communication – using an appropriate greeting, speaking clearly, using correct tone of voice and volume, speaking clearly to people who do not have English as a first language
- Non-verbal communication – smiling, making eye contact, having open body language and a positive facial expression

Completing communication with the customer

`Studied ☐`

- Thanking the customer
- Using appropriate tone of voice and displaying positive body language
- Using an appropriate form of address, e.g. sir, madam
- Use of the customer's name if addressing a regular customer
- Offering further assistance or support

Knowledge recap

1. Why is it most important for a reception area to be clean and tidy?

2. What non-verbal skills are required by someone working in customer service?

Topic B.3 Developing customer service skills

To be successful a business will need to ensure that customers receive an excellent service. Complaints should be taken seriously and never ignored. If the issues are dealt with and resolved quickly, the customer's trust in the business will be restored and they will remain loyal.

Communication methods

Studied ☐

There are different ways a customer could contact a business and these include visiting the premises, where all communication will be face to face, contacting the business by telephone or in writing by letter or email. It is important that all communications, whether written or spoken, are clear and professional.

Dealing with customer queries

Studied ☐

A salesperson needs to display positive and appropriate body language and must always be polite and patient, especially when dealing with customer queries or complaints. The salesperson will need to demonstrate they are listening to the customer, understanding and empathising, but never disagreeing.

How to deal with customer problems and complaints

Studied ☐

When problems do arise it is important that customers are kept informed and regularly updated on the progress. It is important that any problem is dealt with and resolved quickly. The way the business deals with problems and complaints will be remembered by customers and could be the reason they remain loyal. A business may have introduced a clear policy for resolving customer complaints such as offering an exchange, alternative product or refund. Some businesses escalate all complaints to a manager to deal with. Employees need to know, understand and follow the procedure.

Customer types

Studied ☐

All customers are important and each customer should be treated as an individual. Anyone responsible for customer service should be able to recognise when customers, such as the elderly or people with disabilities, require additional support or help. Customers can sometimes be rude, angry, difficult or even abusive and although rude behaviour is difficult to ignore, it is important that the salesperson remains calm. The customer will want someone to listen to their problems and an apology will always help.

When customers have purchased products that require installation or setting up, it is important that technical information and support is accessible and user-friendly.

Different situations

Studied ☐

Providing effective customer service will not just comprise taking payments or packing products securely but may also involve giving information about the products and services available, demonstrating the product, promoting additional products or services, giving advice and taking and relaying messages for colleagues or managers.

Other customer service skills

Studied ☐

Customer service will require excellent communication skills. An employee who works in a customer service role may also be responsible for:

- keeping records of customer purchases, refunds, complaints
- dealing with problems
- handling complaints
- implementing remedial measures
- emergency situations, such as fire drills or wet floors.

Complying with organisational/business policy

Studied ☐

All employees need to be aware of and comply with policies and procedures implemented by the organisation or business. Anyone responsible for dealing with customer service will need to know their business's policy regarding:

- **complaints procedure** – how to deal with and log customer complaints
- **disclaimers** – what the business is not responsible for, such as customers parking in the business car park
- **service specification statements** – the level of service the business offers and what customers can expect to receive.

Knowledge recap ✓

1. Senior managers are concerned about the service provided for customers. What could they do?

2. What written communications could be sent to customers?

Topic B.4 Limits of authority

It is important that all employees fully understand their job role and the authority they have in the workplace. It is especially important that all employees know the limits of their authority when dealing with customers' queries and complaints. A customer will be extremely annoyed if an employee promises a refund to then discover it is not the company's policy to offer refunds. There can be legal implications if this happens, especially if the customer has bought the product on the understanding that a refund was available.

In all businesses there are managers, team leaders and supervisors who will have authority over some or all of the workplace procedures. To ensure that the business runs smoothly, workplace policies and procedures should clearly define which members of staff are responsible for which areas and who has authority for what. All employees should be aware of these policies.

Service deliverer

Studied ☐

A salesperson or any employee who is responsible for customer service may have limited authority to make the decision to refund or replace faulty items. These employees may have no authority or limited authority on when to offer customers free products and it is their responsibility to check with line managers about the correct action to take.

Line manager/supervisor

Studied ☐

A line manager or supervisor will have greater authority than the sales staff and will be able to authorise refunds for faulty or unwanted products. They may also be able to authorise discounts or free goods. They will be responsible for supervising employees at a lower level and for ensuring that policies and procedures are implemented effectively.

Management

Studied ☐

Managers will have control of the day-to-day functions in the branch or business. They will be allowed to authorise special or exceptional changes to normal procedures and policies.

Knowledge recap

1. Who would be responsible for making changes to workplace policies or procedures?

2. Why is it important for shop staff to know the limit of their authority?

Assessment guidance for learning aim B

2B.P5 **Describe how a selected business meets the needs and expectations of three different types of customer**

✍ **Learner answer**

> I have used The Rink leisure centre because I did my work placement there. There are lots of different departments at The Rink, such as front of house, sports staff and trainers, admin, personnel and marketing staff.
>
> The customers are a young family using the ice rink, a woman from admin support, and a young man in a wheelchair who regularly uses the gym facilities.

Assessor report: The command verb for 2B.P5 is **describe**. To achieve this, the learner will need to give a clear description of how the business meets all of the needs and expectations of its three chosen customers.

The learner has set the scene by correctly identifying the selected business and the three different types of customers.

> The first customer is an external customer who came to The Rink for the first time. The customer was a dad with two children who wanted to use the ice rink.
>
> When the family came to the reception they were told about the opening times for the ice rink and the price. The dad was told about buying a family ticket because it was cheaper and this was cheaper than the dad thought he would have to pay.
>
> The family had never been before so they were given a tour of The Rink and told where toilets, refreshments, the ice rink, changing rooms and lockers were. The family found this useful because they did not have to find their own way.
>
> Before they could skate the family were told about the rules and given a small leaflet to read about what to do and what not to do. The ice rink staff helped in checking that the boots for the children

were the right size and that they were laced correctly. This would prevent the children from hurting their feet. The family enjoyed their skating and the dad thanked the staff for their help.

Assessor report: The learner has clearly described how the family's needs and expectations were met during their first visit to The Rink. To achieve 2B.P5 the learner will now need to provide similar evidence for the other two customers.

The second customer is an external customer who is in a wheelchair and regularly goes to The Rink to use the gym. The outer doors open automatically so the man can get access to the reception area. The reception staff suggested that the man used the lift to the first-floor gym because this is the quieter gym. There is a special chair on the first floor just in case there is a fire and the lift cannot be used.

When the man first came to the gym he was given information about using each piece of equipment. The man was assessed, the same as all customers, by a trainer before he was allowed to use the equipment. The man is offered support when using the equipment and in getting refreshments from the café. The man must be happy with The Rink because he visits several times a week.

Assessor report: The learner has again described how the man's needs and expectations are met during his visit to the gym. The learner now needs to provide evidence for the third customer, the woman in admin support (an internal customer).

Assessor report – overall

Is the evidence sufficient to satisfy the grading criterion?

The learner has produced good descriptions on how two customers' needs and expectations are met and will need to provide similar evidence for the internal customer.

What additional evidence, if any, is required?

To achieve 2B.P5 the learner will need to describe the needs and expectations for the internal customer.

2B.P6 Describe, using examples, the limits of authority that would apply when delivering customer service

✍ Learner answer

> It is important that all staff know the limit to their authority when dealing with refunds or exchanging goods. If staff do not know or understand what they need to do or when they have to ask someone in authority, they make the wrong decision. If their decision is wrong, a customer could get a refund when they should not have received one. The customer will be happy but the managers will not.

Assessor report: The command verb for 2B.P6 is **describe**. To achieve this, the learner will need to give a clear description, with examples, of the limits of authority that would apply when delivering customer service.

The learner has correctly identified why the limits of authority are important and now needs to provide some examples to help describe the limits of authority that would apply when delivering customer service.

> It is important for all staff to know when they can replace or refund goods returned by customers and when they should ask someone in a higher job role or with more authority.
>
> ### Example 1
>
> A customer returned a kettle that was not working and was refused a refund or a new product. The customer was annoyed and contacted the manager to complain. A member of the sales team did not have the authority to do a refund so just told the customer that they could not exchange the kettle.
>
> The member of staff should have asked someone in authority, their line manager, if they should exchange the kettle for a new one or refund the customer's money. The member of staff would be following procedure and the customer would be happy.

Assessor report: The learner has described one example of the limits of authority that would apply when delivering customer service. To achieve 2B.P6 the learner will need to provide more examples.

Sales staff should always ask if they are not sure what to do and should never offer free products or extras unless they have the authority to do so.

Example 2

When a customer orders a large piece of furniture, such as a bed, it may be the business's policy to offer free delivery, but only in the local area.

The customer needs the bed to be delivered but lives just outside the area and does not want to pay the extra for delivery. The salesperson does not want to lose the sale so contacts the line manager to find out if it is possible to authorise the free delivery. The salesperson has followed the correct procedure by getting authority to allow the free delivery. The customer is happy and will use the business again and the managers are happy because the sale was made.

Assessor report: The learner has described, using a good, clear example, how the salesperson knew the limit of their authority and what needed to be done to keep the customer happy and to secure the sale.

The learner has provided two good examples, but to achieve 2B.P6 should include a third example, which focuses on dealing with unusual, extreme or complex requests.

Assessor report – overall

Is the evidence sufficient to satisfy the grading criterion?

The evidence submitted by the learner is good, but both the examples given have been for straightforward problems and the assessment guidance does suggest ways to deal with unusual, extreme or complex requests. The learner should produce a third example which focuses on a customer requiring technical support or a customer wanting a refund on an item they just did not like but for which they have no receipt and which they bought some time ago.

What additional evidence, if any, is required?

To achieve 2B.P6 the learner will need to describe a third example which focuses on dealing with unusual, extreme or complex requests.

2B.P7 Demonstrate effective communication skills to meet customer needs when dealing with three different customer types in customer service situations

✍ Learner answer

I have used my work placement at The Rink for 2B.P7. My first customer wanted to let us know about the wet floor in the washrooms. My second customer is new to The Rink, in a wheelchair and wants to join the gym. My third customer is an internal customer who wants up-to-date figures on new customers.

My line manager at The Rink completed the observation statements.

Assessor report: The command verb for 2B.P7 is **demonstrate**, which is to provide several examples or related evidence which clearly support the arguments you are making. This may include showing practical skills. To achieve 2B.P7 the learner will have to demonstrate effective communication skills for three different customer service situations.

The learner has clearly identified the three customer service situations which will be used to generate the evidence for 2B.P7.

I have attached the observation document from my line manager.

Observation record: The Rink	
Learner name:	Jane White
Assessor name:	Tom Press
Qualification:	Edexcel BTEC Level 2 First Award in Business
Unit:	Unit 4: Principles of Customer Service
Description of activity and grading criterion	

2B.P7 – Demonstrate effective communication skills to meet customer needs when dealing with three different customer types in customer service situations.

Jane is working in a receptionist job role at The Rink and was observed demonstrating her communication skills with three customers.

What the learner did

A customer wanted to let Jane know about the wet floor in the washrooms.

Jane is creating a good image for The Rink and looks very smart in the uniform and her hairstyle is neat and tidy [a].

How the learner met the requirements of the grading criterion
20/09/2012 – A lady approached Jane to inform her about an issue in the washroom. Jane smiled and greeted the customer by name (b) and then asked her about the problem. Jane maintained good eye contact (c) with the customer and made a note of the problem in the complaint log book. Making a log of the incident is the first sign to the customer that the problem is being dealt with. Jane apologised and informed the customer that she would contact maintenance and ask them to resolve the problem. Jane maintained open body language (d) and stood not too close to the customer but close enough to hear what was said. Jane spoke clearly, with an appropriate tone and volume (e).   Jane completed the conversation by apologising again and thanked the customer for reporting the problem (f). Jane promptly contacted maintenance and asked for someone to deal with the problem. The actions taken were also added to the log, with the date and time. Jane followed all the correct procedures for dealing with this problem.

Learner signature:	Jane White
Date:	20/09/2012
Assessor signature:	Tom Press
Date:	20/09/2012

Assessor report: The assessor has produced a detailed observation statement which is correctly personalised and clearly demonstrates how the learner used effective communication skills (for example, being professional and creating a good impression (a), smiling and using an appropriate greeting (b), maintaining eye contact (c), having open body language (d) and speaking with an appropriate tone of voice and at an appropriate volume (e); she also completed the communication by thanking the customer (f)) when dealing with a problem. The observation is signed and dated by both the learner and the assessor. The learner will now need to provide similar evidence for the other two customer types mentioned.

Assessor report – overall

Is the evidence sufficient to satisfy the grading criterion?

The evidence submitted so far for 2B.P7 is very good and the assessor has provided a very detailed description of how the learner demonstrated effective communication skills. The assessor will need to complete the observation for the other two customers.

What additional evidence, if any, is required?

To achieve 2B.P7 the assessor will need to complete the observation and documentation for the second and third customers – the customer in the wheelchair wanting to join the gym and the person looking for figures on new customers.

✍ **Learner answer**

I have used my work placement at The Rink for 2B.M4. There are three problems I had when I worked in the reception area. A customer wanted to use the gym but refused to complete the assessment or the questionnaire. Another customer wanted a refund on their membership because they were moving out of the area and would not be using the centre. Another customer was complaining because the ice rink was closed due to maintenance.

My line manager at The Rink completed the observation statements.

Assessor report: The command verb for 2B.M4 is demonstrate, which means the learner needs to provide several examples or related evidence which clearly support the arguments they are making. This may include showing practical skills. To achieve 2B.M4 the learner will have to demonstrate effective communication skills when dealing with customer problems and complaints.

The learner has clearly identified the two problems and the one complaint which will be used to generate the evidence for 2B.M4.

I have attached my log sheet and the observation by my line manager.

Log sheet			
Date	Problem	Actions taken	Staff name
20/09/2012	A customer requested a refund for the two months left on their membership.	Explained to the customer that the refund policy was for three or more months. Listened to the customer explain why he wanted the refund. Showed the customer where the refund information was recorded in the customer handbook.	**Jane White**
20/09/2012	The customer was getting upset, more upset than annoyed, and requested to speak to a manager.	Explained again the refund policy and informed the customer I would contact the centre manager, who implemented the policy. Contacted the centre manager and provided a brief explanation of the customer request. Informed the centre manager of the information I had given. The centre manager, after a discussion with the customer and me, did agree to the refund. The customer and the manager thanked me for my help and the customer left the centre. The centre manager confirmed I was right about the refund policy, but she gave a discretionary refund to create a caring image of the centre.	**Jane White**

Observation record: The Rink	
Learner name:	Jane White
Assessor name:	Tom Press
Qualification:	Edexcel BTEC Level 2 First Award in Business
Unit:	Unit 4: Principles of Customer Service

Description of activity and grading criterion

2B.M4 – Demonstrate effective communication skills when responding to customer problems and complaints in three customer service situations.

Jane is working in a receptionist job role at The Rink and was observed demonstrating her communication skills when dealing with a problem with a customer.

What the learner did

A customer wanted a refund on their membership because they were moving out of the area and would not be using the centre again. The refund was for two months' membership.

Jane provided the customer with all the correct information and contacted the centre manager when asked to do so.

How the learner met the requirements of the grading criterion
19/09/2012 – Jane greeted the customer by name and with a smile [a]. The customer and Jane briefly discussed the weather before Jane asked if there was a problem. The customer did appear uncomfortable but Jane listened actively and patiently to all the customer had to say [b]. In a positive tone [c] Jane politely informed the customer about The Rink's three-months refund policy and showed the customer where the refund information was recorded in the customer handbook. The customer was becoming a little upset, but Jane remained calm, confirmed that she had fully understood the problem and then confirmed the refund policy at The Rink [d]. Jane maintained eye contact when apologising and explaining in a clear tone [e] that the refund policy was the procedure that all staff had to follow. The customer asked to speak to a senior manager to try to get a refund. Jane contacted the centre manager and explained the problem. The centre manager spoke to Jane and the customer and confirmed that Jane had provided an accurate account of the refund policy, but did eventually agree to the refund. The customer and the centre manager thanked Jane for her help. The centre manager explained to Jane that she was correct about the refund policy.

Learner signature:	Jane White
Date:	19/09/2012
Assessor signature:	Tom Press
Date:	19/09/2012

Assessor report: The log is clear and identifies the actions taken. The observation statement is personalised and demonstrates how the learner used effective communication skills to deal with the problem (greeting the customer appropriately by name and with a smile [a], listening to the customer [b], using a positive tone of voice [c], confirming the service [d] and maintaining eye contact [e], complying with organisational policy and escalating the issue to management). The observation is signed and dated by both the learner and the assessor. The learner has provided evidence for one problem and now needs to provide a further log and observation statement on communicating effectively to deal with an additional problem and complaint before 2B.M4 can be awarded.

Assessor report – overall

Is the evidence sufficient to satisfy the grading criterion?

The evidence submitted so far for 2B.M4 is very satisfactory and the learner has produced a very good log, which is supported by a descriptive observation statement. To achieve 2B.M4 the learner will have to produce a log on how she dealt with the customer who refused to complete the assessment or questionnaire and the customer who was angry about the closure of the ice rink. The assessor will need to support the log with a personalised observation statement.

What additional evidence, if any, is required?

To achieve 2B.M4 the learner will need to produce and submit two additional logs, which are supported by observation statements.

2B.D2 **Evaluate the effectiveness of own customer service skills, justifying areas for improvement**

✎ Learner answer

I enjoyed my work placement at The Rink and know that I have learned a lot of new skills. I know I have strengths in some areas of customer service and weaknesses in others. I am going to list the things I did well, my strengths, and the things I did not do well, my weaknesses, in a table and then justify why I need to improve my weaknesses.

Assessor report: The command verbs here are evaluate and justify. To evaluate, the learner will need to review the evidence they have produced regarding how well they handled the situation and come to a conclusion as to how effective their customer service skills were. To justify areas for improvement they will need to identify the lessons learned and give evidence to support why they think these are areas for improvement.

The learner has correctly set the scene by explaining that their evaluation will focus on the strengths and weaknesses of their customer service skills.

What went well and areas for improvement.

What went well	Areas for improvement
I always try to look smart. I tie my hair back so that it looks tidy.	The work area is cluttered and looks untidy.
I arrived on time to start work and was in the reception area before my shift started.	
I keep up to date with any changes to policies or procedures so that I know the information I give is accurate and correct. I knew the policy on refunds on membership. I knew the procedure for reporting the wet floor and logging the problem. I knew the documents that need to be completed before anyone can use the gym equipment. I knew about the induction and assessment policy for the gym. I knew who to contact for help and the authority I have.	I am uncomfortable in dealing with complaints or customers who are angry. I look for the easiest way to get other people to take over dealing with problems or complaints.

I spoke clearly and was always polite to the customers. I greeted all the customers, smiled and used their names when I could. I used an appropriate tone and volume. I listened to what the customers said so I could identify the problem or what information they needed. I always thanked the customer and apologised when there was a problem.	I felt uncomfortable when customers were complaining.
I kept good eye contact when I was talking to or listening to customers. I remembered to not stand too close but stayed close enough to hear what the customers were saying. I remained calm.	
I supported the customer in the wheelchair and gave all the correct information.	I was not sure how much help to give or offer the customer. I felt I had to justify why I did some things just so that the customer did not think it was because he was in a wheelchair.

Assessor report: The learner has produced an interesting table and has identified strengths and weaknesses. They now need to evaluate the points listed and justify areas for improvement.

I take pride in my appearance because I work in the reception area so I am the first person a customer will meet and I want to create a good, positive image for the customers. I know other people rely on me to be on time so I try to arrive at work 30 minutes early. I try to keep the work area tidy but I know some staff get annoyed about removing my mess. I sometimes forget to put things away and this could be a problem for security.

I manage to create a good impression for myself but not my work area and this will not create a good image for the centre. I need to set aside time to remove outdated resources and organise the area so it is user friendly and creates an image of a well-organised leisure centre [a]. Once unwanted items and boxes are removed, the reception area will be easy to keep tidy.

Assessor report: The learner has taken some of the points from the table and is starting to evaluate them. The learner has identified how first impressions are important and has justified why the reception area should look clean, tidy and organised [a].

I always keep up to date with changes to policies because I will need to pass this information on to customers. I did provide good customer service because I knew the correct information about the refund policy and the documentation required to use the gym. I followed the correct procedure for logging the wet floor and contacted the right department so that the issue could be resolved. I know it is important to follow procedures to protect our customers from getting injured when using the centre. I know the limit of my authority, but I did get a little annoyed when a manager awarded the refund because it made me look as though I was wrong. I feel this will give customers confused messages and I was told that my facial expressions showed that I was not happy.

I provided accurate information about the reasons why the assessment and induction are important before customers use the gym. I did remain calm and patient.

Assessor report: The learner has continued to evaluate some of the points identified in the table and now needs to focus on communication skills. The learner has concentrated on what they did well and needs to look more at their weaknesses, e.g. their reaction to being overruled.

I think my biggest strength was communicating with the customer and listening to their problems. I was never rude and kept good eye contact when both speaking and listening. I think this will help the customer trust me and listen to the information I give. I always greeted the customers and used their names when they were regulars. I was comfortable talking to the customers and used an appropriate tone and volume. The reception area can get noisy, especially when the schoolchildren are there, but I try not to shout.

I was aware that the customer in the wheelchair would need extra support [b] but was not sure if I had given more support than was required [a].

The one part of my job I did not like was dealing with customers who were complaining or angry. Although they made me feel uncomfortable I did try to stay calm. I was pleased when I could pass the issue to another member of staff [a]. I know that there will always be customers who are angry and who complain, but dealing with them is one of my biggest weaknesses [c].

Assessor report: The learner has clearly highlighted what went well but has also briefly made reference to some areas for improvement [a]. To achieve 2B.D2 the learner will need to focus on justifying why these areas should be improved.

Assessor report – overall

Is the evidence sufficient to satisfy the grading criterion?

The evidence submitted so far for 2B.D2 is good and the learner has evaluated what went well during the observation, but they need to justify the areas for improvement. The learner has highlighted that the customer in the wheelchair would require additional support [b] and needs to justify why this is an area for improvement. The learner was not sure what help to give and this could make the customer feel uncomfortable and reluctant to return to the centre. The learner would need to find out what physical and other support should be offered and when so that customers are not embarrassed or uncomfortable. The learner could also find out about the support that is available at the centre for customers with other disabilities. The learner is also unsure about how to deal effectively with complaints and needs to justify why this is an area for improvement [c].

What additional evidence, if any, is required?

To achieve 2B.D2 the learner will need to justify the areas for improvement.

Sample assignment brief for learning aim A

PROGRAMME NAME:	Edexcel BTEC Level 2 First Award in Business
	Unit 4: Principles of Customer Service
	Assignment 1
ASSESSOR:	
INTERIM REVIEW:	
DATE ISSUED:	SUBMISSION DATE:

Learning aims and grading criteria covered in this assignment:

2A.P1 Describe the different types of customer service provided by two selected businesses.

2A.P2 Describe the characteristics of consistent and reliable customer service.

2A.P3 Explain how organisational procedures and legislation contribute to consistent and reliable customer service.

2A.P4 Explain how legislative and regulatory requirements affect customer service in a selected business.

2A.M1 Compare how two selected businesses satisfy customers.

2A.M2 Explain how a selected business attempts to exceed customer expectations.

2A.M3 Compare the impact of legislative and regulatory requirements affecting customer service on a selected business.

2A.D1 Assess the effect of providing consistent and reliable customer service on the reputation of a selected business.

Scenario

You have been given the task of producing two information leaflets on providing effective customer service which can be used for training new sales staff.

The first leaflet will need to highlight why having a consistent and reliable customer service is important for a business. The leaflet should include examples on the customer service provision for two businesses.

The second leaflet will need to focus on providing information on legislative and regulatory requirements.

Task 1

For leaflet one you will need to research the customer service provision for two selected businesses.

The first part of your leaflet is to describe the different types of customer service provided by your two selected businesses.

The next step is to:

Describe the characteristics of consistent and reliable customer service.

The next step is to:

Compare how your two selected businesses satisfy customers.

The next step is to:

Explain how one of your selected businesses attempts to exceed customer expectations.

The final part of leaflet one is to:

Assess the effect of providing consistent and reliable customer service on the reputation of a selected business.

Task 2

Leaflet two will provide guidance for the trainee salespeople.

The first section of leaflet two is to explain how organisational procedures and legislation contribute to consistent and reliable customer service.

The next step is to:

Explain how legislative and regulatory requirements affect customer service in a selected business.

The final part of leaflet two is to:

Compare the impact of legislative and regulatory requirements affecting customer service on a selected business.

Sample assignment brief for learning aim B

PROGRAMME NAME:	Edexcel BTEC Level 2 First Award in Business
	Unit 4: Principles of Customer Service
	Assignment 1
ASSESSOR:	
INTERIM REVIEW:	
DATE ISSUED:	SUBMISSION DATE:

Learning aims and grading criteria covered in this assignment:

2B.P5   Describe how a selected business meets the needs and expectations of three different types of customer.

2B.P6   Describe, using examples, the limits of authority that would apply when delivering customer service.

2B.P7   Demonstrate effective communication skills to meet customer needs when dealing with three different customer types in customer service situations.

2B.M4   Demonstrate effective communication skills when responding to customer problems and complaints in three customer service situations.

2B.D2   Evaluate the effectiveness of own customer service skills, justifying areas for improvement.

Scenario

You have been given the task of producing a poster which describes how a business meets customers' needs and expectations and how employees need to know the limit of their authority. Your poster will be used for training purposes and displayed in the staff rest area.

The second part of this assignment is to demonstrate your customer service skills in your work placement or part-time job and finally to evaluate your performance.

Task 1

Your poster should be designed for a business you know well.

The first part is to describe how your selected business meets the needs and expectations of three different types of customers: an internal customer, an external customer and a customer with special requirements, e.g. a customer whose first language is not English.

The second part is to describe, using examples, the limits of authority that would apply when delivering customer service. You should use three examples from dealing with customer queries, refunds, offering discounts, unusual requests or complex requests. Your examples should clearly highlight when it is necessary to ask for help from someone in authority.

Task 2

This next part of your assignment is to demonstrate and evaluate your customer service skills.

In your work placement or part-time job you will need to:

Demonstrate effective communication skills to meet customer needs when dealing with three different customer types in different customer service situations.

Demonstrate effective communication skills when responding to customer problems and complaints in three customer service situations.

This evidence will be observation statements provided by your work placement manager or the line manager in your part-time job. You will also need to include your plan for dealing with the problems or complaints.

Task 3

You will need to write a report which evaluates the effectiveness of your own customer service skills and justifies areas for improvement. You will need to evaluate how you handled the customer service process and what lessons you have learned.

Knowledge recap answers

Topic A.3, page 4

1. The bus station should provide shelter for customers waiting for buses, together with information and support with reading bus times and working out fares. Depending on the size of the bus station there may be toilets and refreshments.

2. Customers will be provided with a reliable and consistent service. The business and customers will benefit as the service provided will be more efficient because the staff are working towards achieving the same outcome.

Topic A.4, page 6

1. Repeat business – customers will continue to purchase products or service from the business rather than going to competitors. This will lead to more sales and more profit.

2. The bus station managers could ask customers face to face or by questionnaire what they wanted and most would say: staff to help customers find the correct bus stop; user-friendly timetables or staff to provide information on the buses; a clean and tidy environment with warm and sheltered places to sit, rest and wait for buses.

Topic A.5, page 8

1. Managers could observe the staff and then provide them with feedback from their observations. The feedback should identify areas of good practice and areas for development. The business could also introduce supportive training sessions.

2. The business could ask customers to complete a survey or questionnaire or ask for their opinions when they are being served. The business should also review the nature of any complaints.

Topic A.6, page 10

1. A good reputation is established by the business providing customers with a service that meets and satisfies their needs.

2. Customers will become repeat customers and will tell others about the service they have received, which would generate more business. More customers will hopefully increase sales and market share.

Topic A.7, page 12

1. The travel agent should provide excellent customer service and products that are good value for money. The travel agent could introduce a range of discounts, promotions or special offers, or sell products with added value. Added value could be, for example, free in-flight meals, extra luggage allowance, free transfer to hotels.

2. The business could provide information leaflets and all relevant documents, such as invoices, in larger print or braille. The business could provide audio recordings to support written information leaflets.

Topic A.8, page 14

1. The business is responsible for providing a safe and secure environment for employees and customers. The business could get a bad reputation if employees or customers had accidents or were injured while using the business's facilities. The business could face being taken to court by someone who was injured while on the business premises or when using its facilities.

2. The mission statement identifies what the business does and what it will provide for customers.

Topic A.9, page 15

1. The employer is responsible for all of the following: providing a safe and secure environment; training staff; providing all relevant protective clothing and equipment; logging accidents; having sufficiently trained first aiders.

2. The Data Protection Act was introduced to prevent personal details of employees and customers being passed on to a third party without the consent of the person.

Topic B.1, page 35

1. A business will need a positive image to recruit qualified staff and to appeal to customers. Employees will be reluctant to work for a business that has a poor image or a bad reputation. Customers will be reluctant to use a business that has a poor image or a bad reputation.

2. Customers with special requirements could be the elderly, customers with babies or young children, wheelchair users, customers with sight or hearing problems, customers with disabilities, or customers who do not speak English.

Topic B.2, page 36

1. The reception area is the first place visitors or customers will see and it is important to create a good first impression.

2. Non-verbal skills will be smiling, maintaining good eye contact but not staring, not standing too close but standing close enough to hear, appropriate facial expressions.

Topic B.3, page 38

1. Senior managers could ask customers for their feedback on the service provided. They could also observe and monitor the customer service and review the logged complaints. They could act as customers and note how they are treated.

2. A business could send letters, emails, invoices or promotional leaflets to customers.

Topic B.4, page 39

1. Managers or the owner of the business would be responsible for making changes to policies and procedures.

2. It is important for shop staff to know the limit of their authority so that they provide customers with advice and information that is correct. If something is outside of their authority it should be passed on to the relevant member of staff.

Picture credits

The authors and publishers would like to thank the following for the use of photographs in this volume:

Figure 1.1 © .shock – Fotolia; Figure 1.2 © Cultura Creative / Alamy; Figure 1.3 © Monkey Business – Fotolia; Figure 1.4 © Image Source/Corbis; figure 1.4 © Studio DER – Fotolia; Figure 1.5 © seewhatmitchsee – Fotolia; Figure 1.6 © Studio DER – Fotolia; Figure 1.7 © Chad McDermott – Fotolia